# Italian Dialogues for Beginners
# Beginners

## *Book 2*

Over 100 Daily Used Phrases and Short Stories to Learn Italian in Your Car. Have Fun and Grow Your Vocabulary with Crazy Effective Language Learning Lessons

**LEARN LIKE A NATIVE**

**www.LearnLikeNatives.com**

# *TABLE OF CONTENT*

# INTRODUCTION

Before we dive into some Italian, I want to congratulate you, whether you're just beginning, continuing, or resuming your language learning journey. Here at Learn Like a Native, we understand the determination it takes to pick up a new language and after reading this book, you'll be another step closer to achieving your language goals.

As a thank you for learning with us, we are giving you free access to our 'Speak Like a Native' eBook. It's packed full of practical advice and insider tips on how to make language learning quick, easy, and most importantly, enjoyable. Head over to LearnLikeNatives.com to access your free guide and peruse our huge selection of language learning resources.

Learning a new language is a bit like cooking—you need several different ingredients and the right technique, but the end result is sure to be delicious. We created this book of short stories for learning Italian because language is alive. Language is about the senses—hearing, tasting the words on your tongue, and touching another culture up close. Learning a language in a classroom is a fine place to start, but it's not a complete introduction to a language.

In this book, you'll find a language come to life. These short stories are miniature immersions into the Italian language, at a level that is perfect for beginners. This book is not a lecture on grammar. It's not an endless vocabulary list. This book is the closest you can come to a language immersion without leaving the country. In the stories within, you will see people speaking to each other, going through daily life situations, and using the most common, helpful words and phrases in language.

You are holding the key to bringing your Italian studies to life.

## Made for Beginners

We made this book with beginners in mind. You'll find that the language is simple, but not boring. Most of the book is in the present tense, so you will be able to focus on dialogues, root verbs, and understand and find patterns in subject-verb agreement.

This is not "just" a translated book. While reading novels and short stories translated into Italian is a wonderful thing, beginners (and even novices) often run into difficulty. Literary licenses and complex sentence structure can make reading in your second language truly difficult—not to mention BORING. That's why Italian Short

Stories for Beginners is the perfect book to pick up. The stories are simple, but not infantile. They were not written for children, but the language is simple so that beginners can pick it up.

## The Benefits of Learning a Second Language

If you have picked up this book, it's likely that you are already aware of the many benefits of learning a second language. Besides just being fun, knowing more than one language opens up a whole new world to you. You will be able to communicate with a much larger chunk of the world. Opportunities in the workforce will open up, and maybe even your day-to-day work will be improved.

Improved communication can also help you expand your business. And from a neurological perspective, learning a second language is like taking your daily vitamins and eating well, for your brain!

## How To Use The Book

The chapters of this book all follow the same structure:

- A short story with several dialogs
- A summary in Italian
- A list of important words and phrases and their English translation
- Questions to test your understanding
- Answers to check if you were right
- The English translation of the story to clear every doubt

You may use this book however is comfortable for you, but we have a few recommendations for getting the most out of the experience. Try these tips and if they work for you, you can use them on every chapter throughout the book.

1) Start by reading the story all the way through. Don't stop or get hung up on any particular words or phrases. See how much of the plot you can understand in this way. We think you'll get a lot more of it than you may expect, but it is completely normal not to understand everything in the story. You are learning a new language, and that takes time.

2) Read the summary in Italian. See if it matches what you have understood of the plot.

3) Read the story through again, slower this time. See if you can pick up the meaning of any words or phrases you don't understand

11

by using context clues and the information from the summary.

4) Test yourself! Try to answer the five comprehension questions that come at the end of each story. Write your answers down, and then check them against the answer key. How did you do? If you didn't get them all, no worries!

5) Look over the vocabulary list that accompanies the chapter. Are any of these the words you did not understand? Did you already know the meaning of some of them from your reading?

6) Now go through the story once more. Pay attention this time to the words and phrases you haven't understand. If you'd like, take the time to look them up to expand your meaning of the story. Every time you read over the story, you'll understand more and more.

7) Move on to the next chapter when you are ready.

## Read and Listen

The audio version is the best way to experience this book, as you will hear a native Italian speaker tell you each story. You will become accustomed to their accent as you listen along, a huge plus for when you want to apply your new language skills in the real world.

If this has ignited your language learning passion and you are keen to find out what other resources are available, go to LearnLikeNatives.com, where you can access our vast range of free learning materials. Don't know where to begin? An excellent place to start is our 'Speak Like a Native' free eBook, full of practical advice and insider tips on how to make language learning quick, easy, and most importantly, enjoyable.

And remember, small steps add up to great advancements! No moment is better to begin learning than the present.

# FREE BOOK!

Get the *FREE BOOK* that reveals the secrets path to learn any language fast, and without leaving your country.

## Discover:

- The language 5 golden rules to master languages at will

- Proven mind training techniques to revolutionize your learning

- A complete step-by-step guide to conquering any language

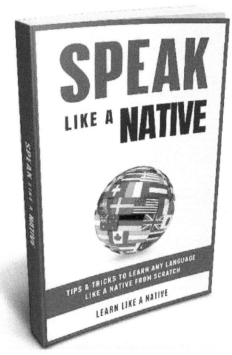

# CHAPTER 1
# John's Homework / School
# + Classroom

La Signora Freschi è una **maestra** di quarta elementare. Insegna alla **scuola** elementare di Cantù. La scuola è in un edificio di mattoni rossi. È in una piccola città.

La Signora Freschi ha una **classe** di 15 **studenti**. I suoi studenti sono bambini e bambine. Di solito sono bravi studenti. La Signora Freschi ha una routine. I suoi studenti iniziano la giornata ai loro **banchi**, seduti sulle loro **sedie**. La Signora Freschi chiama l'appello.

"Luisa?" esclama.

"Presente!" grida Luisa.

"Michele?" dice la Signora Freschi.

"Presente", risponde Michele.

"Giovanni?"

"Sono qui, Signora Freschi," dice Giovanni.

E così via. Dopo l'appello, La Signora Freschi inizia la giornata con la **matematica**. Per i suoi studenti, la matematica è difficile. La classe ascolta La Signora Freschi insegnare. Guardano mentre scrive sulla **lavagna**. A volte, uno studente risolve un problema di fronte alla classe. Usano il **gesso** per scrivere la soluzione. Gli altri studenti fanno gli esercizi nei loro **quaderni**.

Il momento preferito di tutti è l'ora di pranzo. La classe si avvia verso la mensa. Hanno due scelte. Un'opzione è un pasto sano di carne e verdure. L'altra scelta è pizza o hamburger. Alcuni studenti portano un pranzo da casa.

Nel pomeriggio, studiano la storia. Il venerdì, hanno lezione di **scienze** in **laboratorio**. Fanno diversi **esperimenti**, ad esempio come coltivare piante da un pezzo di patata.

La Signora Freschi dà ai suoi studenti **compiti** a casa ogni giorno. Portano i compiti a casa e li svolgono la sera. Il giorno dopo, li portano a scuola. L'unica giustificazione valida per i compiti incompleti è un biglietto dei genitori.

Un giorno, la classe esamina i compiti di **inglese** insieme.

"Per favore, portate tutti i vostri **compiti** sulla mia cattedra", dice La Signora Freschi. Tutti portano i loro compiti alla Signora Freschi. Tutti tranne Giovanni.

"Giovanni, dove sono i tuoi compiti?" dice La Signora Freschi.

Il volto di Giovanni è molto rosso. È nervoso.

"Non li ho", dice Giovanni.

"Hai una giustificazione scritta dei tuoi genitori?" chiede La Signora Freschi.

"No", risponde Giovanni.

"Perché non hai fatto i compiti, allora?" chiede la Signora Freschi. Giovanni dice qualcosa sottovoce..

"Cosa? Non ti sentiamo", dice la Signora Freschi. Fa un sorriso gentile a Giovanni. Sembra nervoso.

"Il mio cane mi ha mangiato i compiti", dice Giovanni. e gli altri studenti ridono. Questa scusa è la classica scusa per non aver fatto i compiti.

"È nel tuo **zaino**? O forse nel tuo **armadietto**?" chiede la Signora Freschi. Vuole aiutare Giovanni.

"No, il mio cane l'ha mangiato!" insiste Giovanni.

"Questa è la **scusa più vecchia del mondo**", dice la Signora Freschi.

"È vero!" dice Giovanni. Giovanni è un bravo studente. Di solito prende sempre 10. La Signora Freschi non vuole mandare Giovanni **nell'ufficio del preside** per aver mentito. Non crede a Giovanni, ma decide di dargli un'altra possibilità.

"Porta i compiti domani," dice la Signora Freschi. "Ecco un'altra copia." Giovanni prende il **foglio dei compiti** e ringrazia la Signora Freschi. La classe torna sul quaderno di arte. Oggi, nell'ora di arte, stanno disegnando un quadro con **matite** colorate. Gli studenti amano l'ora di arte. È un'occasione per rilassarsi. Disegnano e disegnano fino a quando suona la **campanella**. La scuola è finita.

Gli studenti parlano nei corridoi. Si scambiano appunti. Gli studenti della classe di quarta, aspettano fuori. I loro genitori li prendono. Alcuni di loro sono a piedi. Altri sono in auto. Gli insegnanti li aiutano a trovare i loro genitori.

La Signora Freschi finisce il suo lavoro e mette il **portatile** nella sua borsa. La sua classe è pulita e vuota. Esce. Mentre cammina verso la sua auto, vede Giovanni e suo padre. Il padre di Giovanni lo viene a prendere ogni giorno con il loro cane. La Signora Freschi saluta Giovanni e suo padre.

"Ciao, Giovanni!" dice La Signora Freschi.

"Buon pomeriggio, Signora Freschi," dice Giovanni.

"È questo il cane che ti ha mangiato i compiti?" chiede La Signora Freschi. Sorride, così Giovanni sa che lo sta prendendo in giro.

"Sì, Signora Freschi," dice il padre di Giovanni. "Grazie per la comprensione. Giovanni era così preoccupato di mettersi nei guai!"

La Signora Freschi è scioccata! Questa volta, il cane ha davvero mangiato i compiti di Giovanni!

## RIASSUNTO

La Signora Freschi insegna a una classe di quarta elementare. Il suo studente Giovanni non ha con sé i compiti che doveva fare a casa. Dice che il cane li ha mangiati. La maestra pensa che Giovanni stia mentendo. Dopo la scuola La Signora Freschi vede Giovanni e suo padre. Il padre di Giovanni conferma la storia di Giovanni sul cane.

## LISTA DI VOCABOLI

| | |
|---|---|
| Professore/Professoressa | teacher |
| Scuola | school |
| Classe | class |
| Stundenti | students |
| Banco | desk |
| Sedia | chair |
| Appello | roll call |
| Matemática | math |
| Lavagna | blackboard |

| | |
|---|---|
| Gessetto | chalk |
| Cuaderno | notebook |
| Storia | history |
| Scienze | science |
| Laboratorio | lab |
| Esperimento | experiment |
| Compito | homework |
| Inglese | English |
| Fogli | papers |
| Zaino/Cartella | backpack |
| Armadietto | locker |

| | |
|---|---|
| La scusa più vecchia del mondo | the oldest excuse in the book |
| Ottimi voti | straight A's |
| Ufficio del preside | principal's office |
| Foglio di lavoro | worksheet |
| Matita | pencils |
| Campanella | bell |
| Laptop | laptop |

**DOMANDE**

1) Come comincia la giornata nella classe della Signora Freschi?

    a) gli studenti si alzano e gridano

    b) con un compito a casa

    c) con l'appello

    d) con le urla della Signora Freschi

2) Qual è il momento preferito di tutti gli alunni della quarta elementare di Cantù?

    a) L'appello

    b) Il momento del pranzo

    c) L'ora di matematica

    d) Dopo che suona la campana

3) Perché la Signora freschi dice che la scusa di Giovanni è la più vecchia del mondo?

    a) perché tutti gli studenti usano quella scusa

    b) perché Giovanni è il più vecchio della classe

    c) perché ha dimenticato il suo libro rosso

    d) perché il suo cane ha sette anni

4) Cosa devi avere se non fai i compiti?

    a) un esperimento scientifico

    b) una buona scusa

    c) niente, va bene così

    d) una giustificazione scritta dai tuoi genitori

5) Perché la Signora Freschi è sorpresa alla fine della storia?

a) Si rende conto che Giovanni stava dicendo la verità

b) Il cane di Giovanni è in realtà un cavallo

c) Giovanni non le parla

d) Il padre di Giovanni assomiglia a Giovanni

**RISPOSTE**

1) Come comincia la giornata nella classe della Signora Freschi?

c) con l'appello

2) Qual è il momento preferito di tutti gli studenti della quarta elementare di Cantù?

b) Il momento del pranzo

3) Perché la Signora Freschi dice che la scusa di Giovanni è la più vecchia del mondo?

a) perché tutti gli studenti usano quella scusa

4) Cosa devi avere se non fai i compiti?

d) una giustificazione scritta dai tuoi genitori

5) Perché la Signora freschi è sorpresa alla fine della storia?

a) si rende conto che Giovanni stava dicendo la verità

# *Translation of the Story*

## John's Homework

STORY

Mrs. Kloss is a grade 4 **teacher**. She teaches at Homewood Elementary School. The **school** is in a red brick building. It is in a small town.

Mrs. Kloss has a **class** of 15 students. Her **students** are boys and girls. They are usually good students. Mrs. Kloss has a routine. Her students start the day at their **desks**, seated in their **chairs**. Mrs. Kloss calls **roll call**.

"Louise?" she says.

"Here!" shouts Louise.

"Mike?" says Mrs. Kloss.

"Present," says Mike.

"John?"

"Here, Mrs. Kloss," John says.

And so on. After roll call, Mrs. Kloss starts the day with **math**. For her students, math is difficult. The class listens to Mrs. Kloss teach. They watch as she writes on the **blackboard**. Sometimes, one student solves a problem in front of the class. They use **chalk** to write out the solution. The other students do the problems in their **notebooks**.

Everyone's favorite time is lunch time. The class goes to the lunchroom. They have two choices. One choice is a healthy meal of meat and vegetables. The other choice is pizza or hamburgers. Some students bring a lunch from home.

In the afternoon, they study **history**. On Fridays, they have **science** class in the **lab**. They do **experiments**, like growing plants from a piece of potato.

Mrs. Kloss gives her students **homework** every day. They take the work home. They work at night. The next day, they bring it to school. The only excuse for incomplete homework is a note from their parents.

One day, the class reviews the **English** homework together.

"Everyone, please bring your **papers** to my desk," says Mrs. Kloss. Everyone brings their homework to Mrs. Kloss. Everyone except for John.

"John, where is your homework?" says Mrs. Kloss.

John's face is very red. He is nervous.

"I don't have it," says John.

"Do you have a note from your parents?" asks Mrs. Kloss.

"No," says John.

"Why didn't you do your homework, then?" asks Mrs. Kloss. John says something very quietly.

"What? We can't hear you," says Mrs. Kloss. She gives John a kind smile. He looks nervous.

"My dog ate my homework," says John. Mrs. Kloss and the other students laugh. This excuse is the most typical excuse for not having work done.

"Is it in your **backpack**? Or maybe your **locker**?" asks Mrs. Kloss. She wants to help John.

"No, my dog ate it!" insists John.

"That's the **oldest excuse in the book**," says Mrs. Kloss.

"It is true!" says John. John is a good student. He usually makes **straight A's**. Mrs. Kloss does not want to send Jon to the **principal's office** for lying. She does not believe John, but she decides to give him another chance.

"Bring the homework tomorrow," says Mrs. Kloss. "Here is another copy." John takes the **worksheet** and thanks Mrs. Kloss. The class turns to their **art** notebook. Today in art class they are drawing a picture with colored **pencils**. Students love art class. It is a chance to relax. They draw and draw until the **bell** rings. School is over.

Students talk in the hallways. They exchange notes. The Grade 4 students wait outside. Their parents pick them up. Some of them are on foot. Some of them are in cars. The teachers help them to find their parents.

Mrs. Kloss finishes her work. She packs her **laptop** into her bag. Her classroom is clean and empty. She goes outside. As she walks to her car, she see John and his dad. John's father picks him up with their dog. Mrs. Kloss waves to John and his father.

"Hello, John!" says Mrs. Kloss.

"Good afternoon, Mrs. Kloss," John says.

"Is this the dog that ate your homework?" asks Mrs. Kloss. She smiles, so John knows she is teasing.

"Yes, Mrs. Kloss," says John's father. "Thank you for understanding. John is so worried about getting in trouble!"

Mrs. Kloss is shocked! This time, the dog really did eat the homework.

# CHAPTER 2
# Thrift Store Bargain / house and furniture

STORIA

Luisa e Maria sono migliori amiche. Sono anche **coinquiline**. Condividono un **appartamento** nel centro della città. Oggi vogliono acquistare **mobili** per la loro **casa**. Luisa e Maria sono entrambe studentesse. Non hanno molti soldi.

"Dove possiamo fare shopping?" chiede Luisa a Maria.

"Abbiamo bisogno di molti mobili", dice Maria. È preoccupata per i soldi.

"Lo so," dice Luisa. "Dobbiamo trovare un **affare**."

"Ho un'idea. Andiamo al negozio dell'usato!" dice Maria.

"Ottima idea!" dice Luisa.

Le due ragazze guidano l'auto fino al negozio dell'usato. Si tratta di un negozio molto grande. L'edificio è più grande di dieci **case**.

Le ragazze parcheggiano l'auto. Il parcheggio è vuoto.

"Wow", dice Luisa. "Il negozio è molto grande."

"Assolutamente", dice Maria. "E qui non c'è nessuno."

"Saremo le uniche", dice Luisa. "Possiamo **fare come a casa nostra**."

Le ragazze entrano nel negozio. Il negozio ha qualsiasi cosa. A destra, c'è la sezione **cucina**. Ci sono alti **frigoriferi** e vecchi forni a **microonde** sugli **scaffali**. Ci sono **tostapane** di tutti i colori. I prezzi sono buoni. Un forno a microonde costa solo $ 10.

Tutto è un affare. Gli articoli sono usati e di seconda mano. Tuttavia, Maria e Luisa devono trovare oggetti che le piacciono. Ci sono più di una dozzina di divani. Maria e Luisa hanno bisogno di un **divano**. Passano il tempo a parlare dei diversi divani. A Maria piace un divano in pelle marrone. A Luisa piace un grande divano viola. Sono indecise. Luisa vede una **sedia** viola. Le ragazze decidono di prendere il divano viola e la sedia in modo che si abbinino. È perfetto per la loro casa.

"Ho bisogno di un **letto** per la mia **camera da letto**", dice Luisa.

Le ragazze camminano verso la zona notte. Ma prima, attraversano la sezione di arte.

"Sai, abbiamo bisogno di qualcosa per le **pareti**", dice Luisa. Maria è d'accordo. Ci sono grandi

**quadri**, piccoli quadri, **cornici** vuote e fotografie incorniciate. Luisa è attratta da un grande dipinto astratto. Ha linee di vernice rossa, blu e nera.

"Posso dipingere anch'io così", dice Maria. "Sembra un dipinto fatto da dei bambini."

"Sono solo cinque dollari", dice Luisa.

"Oh, va bene!" dice Maria.

Le ragazze finiscono lo shopping. Luisa trova anche una **lampada** per la sua camera da letto. La sua camera da letto è troppo scura. Maria sceglie un **tappeto** per il **bagno**. Le ragazze sono molto felici. Hanno speso solo $ 100 dollari per tutti i mobili.

"Ecco perché fare shopping al negozio dell'usato è un affare", dice Luisa.

"Sì, abbiamo **tutto tranne il lavello della cucina!**" dice Maria.

Maria e Luisa hanno organizzato una festa nel loro appartamento quella sera. E 'una festa per accogliere gli amici. Maria e Luisa vogliono mostrare loro i nuovi mobili.

Il campanello suona. Maria apre la **porta**. Nicola è il primo ad arrivare. Nicola è amico di Maria ed è anche uno studente. Studia storia dell'arte.

"Ciao, ragazze," dice Nicola. "Grazie per avermi invitato."

"Entra, Nicola!" dice Maria. Nicola entra **nell'atrio**. Lei lo abbraccia.

"Vuoi vedere la nostra nuove cose?" chiede Luisa.

"Sì!" disse Nicola.

Luisa e Maria fanno fare il giro dell'appartamento a Nicola. Sono contente del loro **soggiorno**. Il nuovo divano, la sedia e il quadro ci stanno molto bene.

"Tutto questo viene dal negozio dell'usato", dice Maria. È orgogliosa.

Nicola si avvicina al dipinto. "Mi piace molto questo quadro", dice.

"Anche me", dice Luisa. "L'ho scelto io."

"Mi ricorda Jackson Pollock", dice Nicola.

"Chi è Jackson Pollock?" chiede Maria.

"È un pittore molto famoso," dice Nicola. "Schiaccia la pittura sulla tela. Proprio come questo." Nicola guarda attentamente il dipinto.

"È firmato?" chiede. Luisa scuote la testa no. "Guardiamo dietro."

Prendono il dipinto dalla cornice e lo girano. Sono tutti silenziosi. In basso c'è una firma che assomiglia a 'Jackson Pollock'.

"Quanto l'hai pagato?" chiede Nicola.

"Circa cinque dollari", dice Luisa.

"Questo dipinto probabilmente vale almeno $10 milioni di dollari," dice Nicola. Egli è scioccato. Maria guarda Luisa. Luisa guarda Maria.

"Qualcuno vuole un bicchiere di champagne?" dice Maria.

Questo sì che è un affare!

## RIASSUNTO

Maria e Luisa sono in cerca di mobili per la loro nuova casa. Vanno al negozio dell'usato visto che non hanno molti soldi. Comprano molti oggetti. Luisa sceglie un dipinto. Quella sera, ad una festa, il loro amico Nicola vede il dipinto. C'è una sorpresa inaspettata per le ragazze.

## LISTA DI VOCABOLI

| | |
|---|---|
| Coinquilini | roommates |
| Appartamento | apartment |
| Mobuli | furniture |
| Casa | Home/house |
| Offerta / Affare | bargain |

| | |
|---|---|
| Negozio dell'usato | thrift store |
| Fare come a casa nostra | make ourselves at home |
| Cucina | kitchen |
| Frigoriferi | refrigerators |
| Micronde | microwaves |
| Scaffali | shelves |
| Tostapane | toasters |
| Sedia | chair |
| Tavolo | table |
| Divano | sofa |

| | |
|---|---|
| Letto | bed |
| Camera da letto | bedroom |
| Pareti | wall |
| Quadro | frame |
| Lampada | lamp |
| Tappeto | carpet |
| Bagno | bathroom |
| Tutto tranne il lavello della cucina | everything but the kitchen sink |
| Porta | door |
| Atrio | foyer |

| Soggiorno | living room |
|-----------|-------------|

**DOMANDE**

1) Perché Maria e Luisa vanno al negozio dell'usato?

    a) Hanno bisogno di soldi.

    b) Hanno bisogno di mobili ma non hanno molti soldi.

    c) Hanno mobili da vendere.

    d) Vogliono divertirsi un po'.

2) Perché i prezzi al negozio dell'usato sono così bassi?

a) È la stagione della vendita.

b) Sta chiudendo.

c) Gli articoli sono di seconda mano.

d) I prezzi sono normali, non bassi.

3) Quale dei seguenti articoli va in cucina?

a) il letto

b) il forno a microonde

c) la doccia

d) il divano

4) Come fa Nicola a sapere così tanto del dipinto?

a) È un commerciante d'arte professionista.

b) Il dipinto appartiene a Nicola.

c) Lui studia arte.

d) Ha letto un libro.

5) Alla fine, Maria e Luisa sono...

a) tristi.

b) sorprese e ricche.

c) arrabbiate con Nicola.

d) troppo stanche per fare una festa.

## RISPOSTE

1) Perché Maria e Luisa vanno al negozio dell'usato?

    a) Hanno bisogno di soldi.

2) Perché i prezzi al negozio dell'usato sono così bassi?

    c) Gli articoli sono di seconda mano.

3) Quale dei seguenti articoli va in cucina?

    b) il microonde

4) Come fa Nicola a sapere così tanto del dipinto?

    c) Lui studia arte.

5) Alla fine, Maria e Luisa sono...

    b) sorprese e ricche.

# *Translation of the Story*

## Thrift Store Bargain

STORY

Louise and Mary are best friends. They are also **roommates**. They share an **apartment** in the center of town. Today they want to shop for **furniture** for their **home**. Louise and Mary are both students. They do not have much money.

"Where can we shop?" Louise asks Mary.

"We need a lot of furniture," Mary says. She is worried about money.

"I know," says Louise. "We need to find a **bargain**."

"I have an idea. Let's go to the thrift store!" says Mary.

"Great idea!" says Louise.

The two girls drive the car to the thrift store. It is a giant store. The building is bigger than ten **houses**.

The girls park the car. The parking lot is empty.

"Wow," says Louise. "The store is very big."

"Totally," says Mary. "And there is nobody here."

"We will be the only people," says Louise. "We can **make ourselves at home.**"

The girls walk into the store. The store has everything. On the right, there is the **kitchen** section. There are tall **refrigerators** and old **microwaves** on the **shelves**. There are **toasters** of all colors. The prices are good. A microwave costs only $10.

Everything is a bargain. The items are used and second-hand. However, Mary and Louise find items that they like. There are more than a dozen sofas. Mary and Louise need a **sofa**. They spend time talking about the different sofas. Mary likes a brown leather sofa. Louise likes a big purple sofa. They cannot decide. Louise sees a purple **chair**. The girls decide to get the purple sofa and chair so that they match. It is perfect for their home.

"I need a **bed** for my **bedroom**," says Louise.

The girls walk to the bedroom area. First, they pass the art section.

"You know, we need something for the **walls**," says Louise. Mary agrees. There are big paintings, small paintings, empty **frames**, and photographs in frames. Louise decides on a big, abstract painting. It has lines of splattered red, blue, and black paint.

"I can paint like that," says Mary. "It looks like a child's painting."

"It's only five dollars," says Louise.

"Oh, ok!" says Mary.

The girls finish shopping. Louise also finds a **lamp** for her bedroom. Her bedroom is too dark.

Mary chooses a **carpet** for the **bathroom**. The girls are very happy. They spend only $100 dollars for all the furniture.

"That is why shopping at the thrift store is a bargain," says Louise.

"Yes, we got **everything but the kitchen sink**!" says Mary.

Mary and Louise have a party in their apartment that night. It is a party to welcome friends. Mary and Louise want to show their new furniture.

The doorbell rings. Mary opens the **door**. Nick is the first to arrive. Nick is Mary's friend. Nick is also a student. He studies art history.

"Hi, ladies," says Nick. "Thank you for inviting me."

"Come in, Nick!" says Mary. Nick steps into the **foyer**. She hugs him.

"Do you want to see our new stuff?" asks Louise.

"Yeah!" says Nick.

Louise and Mary show Nick around the apartment. They are happy with the **living room**. The new sofa, chair and painting looks great.

"All of this is from the thrift store," says Mary. She is proud.

Nick walks up to the painting. "I really like this painting," he says.

"I do too," says Louise. "I chose it."

"It reminds me of Jackson Pollock," says Nick.

"Who is Jackson Pollock?" asks Mary.

"He is a very famous painter," says Nick. "He splashes paint onto canvas. Just like this one." Nick looks closely at the painting.

"Is it signed?" he asks. Louise shakes her head no. "Let's look behind it then."

They take the painting out of the frame and turn it around. They all are quiet. On the bottom is a signature that looks like 'Jackson Pollock'.

"How much did you pay for this?" asks Nick.

"About five dollars," says Louise.

"This is probably worth at least $10 million dollars," says Nick. He is shocked. Mary looks at Louise. Louise looks at Mary.

"Does anyone want a glass of champagne?" says Mary.

Now that is a bargain!

# CHAPTER 3

# The Goat / common present tense verbs

Ollie si sveglia. Il sole splende. Si ricorda che è sabato. Oggi suo padre non **lavora**. Ciò significa che Ollie e suo padre faranno qualcosa insieme. Cosa possono **fare**? Ollie vuole andare al cinema. Vuole anche giocare ai videogiochi.

Ollie ha dodici anni. Va a scuola. Ma sabato non va a scuola. **Usa** il sabato per fare quello che vuole. Suo padre gli lascia decidere. Quindi Ollie vuole fare qualcosa di divertente.

"papàààààà!" **chiama** Ollie. "**Vieni** qui!"

Ollie aspetta.

Suo padre entra nella camera di Ollie.

"Oggi è sabato", **dice** Ollie.

"Lo **so**, figliolo", dice il padre di Ollie.

"Voglio fare qualcosa di divertente!" dice Ollie.

"Anche io", dice papà.

"Cosa possiamo fare?" **chiede** Ollie.

"Cosa vuoi fare?" chiede suo padre.

"Andare al cinema", dice Ollie.

"Andiamo sempre al cinema sabato", dice il padre di Ollie.

"Giocare ai videogiochi", dice Ollie.

"Giochiamo ai videogiochi tutti i giorni!" dice papà.

"Ok, ok", dice Ollie. **Pensa**. Si ricorda del suo insegnante di scuola. Il suo insegnante **dice** agli studenti di stare all'aperto. L'insegnante dice loro che l'aria fresca è buona. A scuola, studiano gli animali. Ollie viene a conoscenza di animali nella giungla, animali nell'oceano e animali nelle fattorie.

Questo è tutto!

"Papà, andiamo in una fattoria!" dice Ollie. Il papà di Ollie pensa che sia una bella idea. Ha sempre voluto **vedere** e toccare gli animali della fattoria.

Prendono la macchina. Il papà di Ollie guida verso la campagna. Vedono un cartello che dice "Fattoria degli animali". Seguono le indicazioni e parcheggiano l'auto.

Ollie e suo padre acquistano i biglietti per entrare. I biglietti costano $5. Lasciano la biglietteria. C'è un grande edificio in legno, è la fattoria. Dietro la fattoria, c'è un campo enorme. Il campo ha alberi, erba, e recinzioni. In ogni recinzione c'è un tipo diverso di animale. Ci sono centinaia di animali.

Ollie è eccitato. Vede polli, cavalli, anatre e maiali. Li tocca e li ascolta. Ollie **fa** il verso di ogni animale. Alle anatre, dice "quack". Ai maiali, dice "oink". Ai cavalli, dice "nay". Ai polli, dice "bok bok". Gli animali fissano Ollie.

Superati gli animali in gabbia, Ollie vede un gregge di pecore. Il papà di Ollie gli dice che le pecore femmine sono chiamate pecore, mentre le pecore maschi sono montoni. Le pecore neonate si chiamano agnelli. Le pecore mangiano l'erba.

"Possono vederci", dice papà.

"Ma loro non ci guardano", dice Ollie.

"Le pecore possono vedere dietro di sé. Non devono girare la testa", dice papà. Il papà di Ollie sa molto sulle pecore.

"Tagliano il pelo alle pecore in primavera," dice il papà, e racconta a Ollie come la lana delle pecore **diventa** maglioni, sciarpe e altri vestiti caldi. Ollie ha un maglione di lana ed è caldo.

Ollie e suo padre camminano intorno al campo. L'erba è verde. Ci sono mucche in un angolo. Una delle mucche mamma, nutre un vitello.

"Sai cosa fanno le mucche, Ollie?" chiede papà.

"Sì! Il latte!" dice Ollie.

"Proprio così", dice papà.

Ollie sente un verso di animale. **Prende** la mano di suo padre. Camminano verso il suono. Arrivano ad un recinto. **Trovano** una capra. La capra ha le corna bloccate nel recinto. La capra si siede a terra. Non si muove. Le sue corna sono tra il legno e non può muoversi. Ollie e suo padre **guardano** la capra.

"Mi dispiace tanto per la capra", dice Ollie. Sembra triste.

"Povera bestiola!" dice il papà.

"Sembra così triste", risponde Ollie.

"Possiamo aiutarla", dice papà.

"Sì!" risponde Ollie.

Si avvicinano alla capra. Ollie è nervoso. Papà dice di non preoccuparsi. Le corna sono bloccate e la capra non gli farà del male. Ollie guarda negli occhi la capra. La **capra ha bisogno** di aiuto. Ollie parla con la capra. **Prova** a fare suoni morbidi. Vuole mantenere la capra calma.

Il papà di Ollie cerca di muovere le corna. Prova il corno destro. Prova il corno sinistro. Non si muovono. Dopo dieci minuti, si **arrendono**.

"Non riesco a farlo", dice il padre di Ollie.

"Sei sicuro?" chiede Ollie.

"Le corna sono bloccate", dice papà.

"Che cosa facciamo?" chiede Ollie.

L'area intorno alla capra è fango. Non c'è più erba. Il papà di Ollie prende un po'd'erba dal terreno e la porta alla capra. La capra mangia l'erba. La capra sembra affamata. L'erba è finita. Ollie prende più erba da dare alla capra. Accarezzano la capra per qualche minuto. La capra sembra riconoscente.

"Diciamolo al proprietario", dice papà.

"Sì", dice Ollie. "Forse possono aiutarla."

Ollie e suo padre vanno alla biglietteria. La biglietteria è un piccolo edificio all'ingresso. Un uomo lavora lì. Ollie e suo padre entrano.

"Salve, signore", dice il padre di Ollie.

"Come posso aiutarvi?" chiede l'uomo.

"C'è una capra", dice il padre di Ollie.

L'uomo interrompe il padre di Ollie. Agita la mano. Sembra annoiato. "Sì, lo sappiamo."

"Sai della capra?" chiede Ollie.

"La capra bloccata nella recinzione?" chiede l'uomo.

"Sì!" dicono Ollie e suo padre.

"Oh sì, quella è Patty," dice l'uomo. "Può uscire quando vuole. Ma le piace avere attenzioni."

Ollie **dà** a suo padre uno sguardo sorpreso. Ollie e suo padre ridono.

"Patty, che capra!" dice Ollie.

## RIASSUNTO

Ollie si sveglia di sabato. Lui e suo padre decidono di fare qualcosa di divertente. Vanno in una fattoria a vedere gli animali. Vedono e toccano molti animali: mucche, cavalli, pecore, e altro ancora. Camminano intorno alla fattoria. È una bella giornata. Trovano una capra intrappolata in un recinto. Cercano di aiutare la capra. La capra è bloccata dalle corna. Gli danno da mangiare dell'erba. Ollie e suo padre vanno a cercare aiuto. L'uomo in biglietteria li ascolta. Dice loro la capra ama ingannare le persone per avere attenzioni. Ollie e suo padre ridono.

## LISTA DI VOCABOLI

| | |
|---|---|
| Lavorare | to work |
| Fare | to do /to make |
| Volere | to want |
| Andare | to go |
| Usare | to use |
| Chiamare | to call |
| Venire | to come |
| Dire | to say |
| Sapere | to know |

| | |
|---|---|
| Chiedere | to ask |
| Pnensare | to think |
| Dire | to tell |
| Vedere | to see |
| Diventare | to become |
| Fare | to make |
| Prendere | to take |
| Incontrare | to find |
| Sentire | to feel |
| Guardare | to look |
| Avere bisogno | to need |

| | |
|---|---|
| Provare | to try |
| Dare | to give |
| Arrendersi | to give up |

## DOMANDE

1) Cosa decidono di fare Ollie e suo padre sabato?

    a) andare al cinema

    b) andare in una fattoria

    c) giocare ai videogiochi

    d) andare a scuola

2) Di quale animale sa molto il padre di Ollie?

    a) pecore

    b) maiali

    c) giraffe

    d) mucche

3) Che cosa succede alla capra?

     a) si nasconde

     b) beve

     c) è incastrata in un recinto

     d) è arrabbiato

4) Cosa fanno Ollie e suo padre per la capra?

     a) la liberano

     b) le danno dell'erba e la accarezzano

     c) chiamano la polizia

     d) le danno un bacio

5) Cosa fa Patty?

     a) lascia la fattoria

b) mangia la spazzatura

c) va alla biglietteria

d) finge di incastrarsi nel recinto per attirare l'attenzione

**RISPOSTE**

1) Cosa decidono di fare Ollie e suo padre sabato?

   b) andare in una fattoria

2) Di quale animale sa molto il padre di Ollie?

   a) pecore

3) Che cosa succede alla capra?

   c) è incastrata in un recinto

4) Cosa fanno Ollie e suo padre per la capra?

   b) le danno dell'erba e la accarezzano

5) Cosa fa Patty?

   d) finge di incastrarsi nel recinto per attirare l'attenzione

# *Translation of the Story*

## The Goat

Ollie wakes up. The sun is shining. He remembers: it is Saturday. Today his dad does not **work**. That means Ollie and his dad **do** something together. What can they do? Ollie **wants** to go to the movies. He also wants to play video games.

Ollie is twelve years old. He goes to school. Saturday he does not go to school. He **uses** Saturday to do what he wants. His dad lets him decide. So Ollie wants to do something fun.

"Daaaaaad!" **calls** Ollie. "**Come** here!"

Ollie waits.

His dad enters Ollie's bedroom.

"Today is Saturday," **says** Ollie.

"I **know**, son," says Ollie's dad.

"I want to do something fun!" says Ollie.

"Me too," says Dad.

"What can we do?" **asks** Ollie.

"What do you want to do?" asks his dad.

"Go to the movies," says Ollie.

"We always go to the movies on Saturday," says Ollie's dad.

"Play video games," says Ollie.

"We play video games everyday!" says Dad.

"Ok, ok," says Ollie. He **thinks**. He remembers his teacher at school. His teacher **tells** the students to go outside. The teacher tells them the fresh air is good. At school, they study animals. Ollie learns about animals in the jungle, animals in the ocean, and animals on farms.

That's it!

"Dad, let's go to a farm!" says Ollie. Ollie's dad thinks that is a great idea. He has always wanted to **see** and touch farm animals.

They take the car. Ollie's dad drives to the countryside. They see a sign that says "Animal Farm". They follow the signs and park the car.

Ollie and his dad buy tickets to enter. Tickets cost $5. They leave the ticket office. There is a big wooden building, the farmhouse. Behind the farmhouse, there is a huge field. The field has trees, grass, and fences. In each fence is a different type of animal. There are hundreds of animals.

Ollie is excited. He sees chickens, horses, ducks, and pigs. He touches them and listens to them. Ollie **makes** a sound to each animal. To the ducks, he says "quack". To the pigs, he says "oink". To the horses, he says "nay". To the chickens, he says "bok bok". The animals stare at Ollie.

Past the animals in cages, Ollie sees a flock of sheep. Ollie's dad tells him that female sheep are called ewes. Male sheep are rams. Baby sheep are called lambs. The sheep are eating grass.

"They can see us," says Dad.

"But they are not looking at us," says Ollie.

"Sheep can see behind themselves. They don't have to turn their heads," says Dad. Ollie's dad knows a lot about sheep.

"They cut the hair on the sheep in spring," says Dad. He tells Ollie how the sheep's wool **becomes** sweaters, scarves and other warm clothing. Ollie has a sweater made of wool. It is warm.

Ollie and his dad walk around the field. The grass is green. There are cows in a corner. One of the mother cows feeds a baby calf.

"You know what cows make, Ollie?" asks Dad.

"Duh! Milk!" says Ollie.

"That's right," says Dad.

Ollie hears an animal sound. He **takes** his dad's hand. They walk towards the sound. They come to a fence. They **find** a goat. The goat has horns stuck in the fence. The goat sits on the ground. It does not move. Its horns are between the wood and it can't move. Ollie and his dad **look** at the goat.

"I feel so bad for the goat," says Ollie. She seems sad.

"Poor guy!" says Dad.

"He looks so sad," says Ollie.

"We can help him," Dad says.

"Yeah!" says Ollie.

They get close to the goat. Ollie is nervous. Dad says not to worry. The horns are stuck and the goat will not hurt them. Ollie looks into the eyes of the goat. The goat **needs** help. Ollie talks to the goat. He **tries** to make soft sounds. He wants to keep the goat calm.

Ollie's dad tries to move the horns. He tries the right horn. He tries the left horn. They don't move. After ten minutes, they **give up**.

"I can't do it," says Ollie's dad.

"Are you sure?" asks Ollie.

"The horns are stuck," says Dad.

"What do we do?" asks Ollie.

The area around the goat is mud. There is no grass left. Ollie's dad takes some grass from the ground and brings it to the goat. The goat eats the grass. The goat looks hungry. The grass is gone. Ollie gets more grass to take to the goat. They pet the goat for a few minutes. The goat seems grateful.

"Let's tell the owner," says Dad.

"Yeah," says Ollie. "Maybe they can help her."

Ollie and his dad go to the ticket office. The ticket office is a small building at the entrance. A man works there. Ollie and his dad go inside.

"Hello, sir," says Ollie's dad.

"How can I help you?" asks the man.

"There's a goat—" says Ollie's dad.

The man interrupts Ollie's dad. He waves his hand. He looks bored. "Yeah, we know."

"You know about the goat?" asks Ollie.

"The goat stuck in the fence?" asks the man.

"Yes!" say Ollie and his dad.

"Oh yes, that's Patty," says the man. "She can get herself out whenever she wants. She just likes the attention."

Ollie **gives** his dad a surprised look. Ollie and his dad laugh.

"Patty, what a goat!" Ollie says.

# CONCLUSION

Y ou did it!

You finished a whole book in a brand new language. That in and of itself is quite the accomplishment, isn't it?

Congratulate yourself on time well spent and a job well done. Now that you've finished the book, you have familiarized yourself with over 500 new vocabulary words, comprehended the heart of 3 short stories, and listened to loads of dialogue unfold, all without going anywhere!

Charlemagne said "To have another language is to possess a second soul." After immersing yourself in this book, you are broadening your horizons and opening a whole new path for yourself.

Have you thought about how much you know now that you did not know before? You've learned everything from how to greet and how to express your emotions to basics like colors and place words. You can tell time and ask question. All without opening a schoolbook. Instead, you've cruised through fun, interesting stories and possibly listened to them as well.

Perhaps before you weren't able to distinguish meaning when you listened to Italian. If you used the audiobook, we bet you can now pick out meanings and words when you hear someone speaking. Regardless, we are sure you have taken an important step to being more fluent. You are well on your way!

Best of all, you have made the essential step of distinguishing in your mind the idea that most often hinders people studying a new language. By approaching Italian through our short stories and dialogs, instead of formal lessons with just grammar and vocabulary, you are no longer in the 'learning' mindset. Your approach is much more similar to an osmosis, focused on speaking and using the language, which is the end goal, after all!

So, what's next?

This is just the first of five books, all packed full of short stories and dialogs, covering essential, everyday Italian that will ensure you master the basics. You can find the rest of the books in the series, as well as a whole host of other resources, at LearnLikeNatives.com. Simply add the book to your library to take the next step in your language learning journey. If you are ever in need of new ideas or direction, refer to our 'Speak Like a Native' eBook, available to you for free at LearnLikeNatives.com, which clearly outlines practical steps you can take to continue learning any language you choose.

We also encourage you to get out into the real world and practice your Italian. You have a leg up on most beginners, after all—instead of pure textbook learning, you have been absorbing the sound and soul of the language. Do not underestimate the foundation you have built reviewing the chapters of this book. Remember, no one feels 100% confident when they speak with a native speaker in another language.

One of the coolest things about being human is connecting with others. Communicating with someone in their own language is a wonderful gift. Knowing the language turns you into a local and opens up your world. You will see the reward of learning languages for many years to come, so keep that practice up!. Don't let your fears stop you from taking the chance to use your Italian.

Just give it a try, and remember that you will make mistakes. However, these mistakes will teach you so much, so view every single one as a small victory! Learning is growth.

Don't let the quest for learning end here! There is so much you can do to continue the learning process in an organic way, like you did with this book. Add another book from Learn Like a Native to your library. Listen to Italian talk radio. Watch some of the great Italian films. Put on the latest CD from Pavarotti. Take cooking lessons in Italian. Whatever you do, don't stop because every little step you take counts towards learning a new language, culture, and way of communicating.

**www.LearnLikeNatives.com**

Learn Like a Native is a revolutionary **language education brand** that is taking the linguistic world by storm. Forget boring grammar books that never get you anywhere, Learn Like a Native teaches you languages in a fast and fun way that actually works!

As an international, multichannel, language learning platform, we provide **books, audio guides and eBooks** so that you can acquire the knowledge you need, swiftly and easily.

Our **subject-based learning**, structured around real-world scenarios, builds your conversational muscle and ensures you learn the content most relevant to your requirements. Discover our tools at *LearnLikeNatives.com*.

When it comes to learning languages, we've got you covered!

Lightning Source UK Ltd.
Milton Keynes UK
UKHW050021050822
406721UK00008B/57